Poems –
Songs and Letters

Poems –
Songs and Letters

Volume II

Keith Vance

POEMS - SONGS AND LETTERS: VOLUME II

This book is written to provide information and motivation to readers. Its purpose is not to render any type of psychological, legal, or professional advice of any kind. The content is the sole opinion and expression of the author, and not necessarily that of the publisher.

Copyright © 2019 by Keith Vance

All rights reserved. No part of this book may be reproduced, transmitted, or distributed in any form by any means, including, but not limited to, recording, photocopying, or taking screenshots of parts of the book, without prior written permission from the author or the publisher. Brief quotations for noncommercial purposes, such as book reviews, permitted by Fair Use of the U.S. Copyright Law, are allowed without written permissions, as long as such quotations do not cause damage to the book's commercial value. For permissions, write to the publisher, whose address is stated below.

Printed in the United States of America.

ISBN   978-1-64552-136-5   (Paperback)
ISBN   978-1-64552-137-2   (Digital)

Lettra Press books may be ordered through booksellers or by contacting:

Lettra Press LLC
18601 Green Valley Ranch Blvd.
Unit 108, Box 204 Denver, CO 80249
1 303 586 1431 | info@lettrapress.com
www.lettrapress.com

Contents

Dedication ix
Major Players x
Introduction xi

"The Awesome Oak"

"AAAAAAAAH!!!" 1
"A Wanderers Heart" 3
"All The Way Down" 4
"An Unfamiliar Place" 6
"Bad Habits" 7
"Bottle Bravery" 8
"Charade" 9
"Cryin' Eyes" 10
"Dirty Kerosene" 12
"Empty Promises And Lonesome Lies" 13
"Every Road I Take" 15
"For A Mother's Love" 17
"For Destiny" 18
"Forty – Forty" 19
"Happy Tears" 21
"Happy With What I've Got" 22
"Hey George" 23
"I Cry" 25
"If You Still Love Me Then" 26
"I'll Sing You A Letter" 28
"In Memory Of" 29
"Justice" 30
"Kathleen, My Kathleen" 31
"Lay Your Lovin' Down" 33
"Life's Perfect Rhyme" 35
"Life's Levy" 36

"Long Way To Dover" 38
"Look At Me" 40
"Lost In Time" 41
"Love" 42
"Loves Weakest Link" 44
"Midnight Memory" 45
"The Midnight Mumbler" 47
"Missing You" 51
"Morbidity" 52
"My Heart" 53
"My One True Love" 54
"Never Alone" 55
"No Desire To Lie To You" 56
"Next To You" 57
"No More Tears Over You" 59
"No Remorse" 61
"The One That Got Away" 63
"North Carolina – 1965" 64
"Ode To Olie James" 65
"Open-Ended" 66
"Poetry's Bleeding Hearts" 67
"Rainbow" 69
"Reaching Out" 70
"Red Vette Blues" 71
"Right The Wrongs" 73
"Roll On Sweet River" 78
"Scrambled" 81
"70's Magic" 83
"Shaking The Dust Off My Feet" 85
"She's A Real Good Friend Of Mine" 86
"She's Special" 87
"Silhouette Sex" 88
"Stop Your Rambling And Runnin' Around" 89
"Taking My Heart Home To Die" 90
"Teenage Fever" 91
"To Gail" 92

"That Empty Feeling" 93
"The Awesome Oak" 94
"The Big-B-Blues" 95
"The Loves Of Mr. V" 100
"The Un-Gambler" 101
"Thee I Love" 105
"They Need Me" 106
"This Land Of "God's", And Ours" 108
"Tired Of Being So Accused" 109
"Think Of The Memory's" 111
"This "Ole" Show" 112
"Three Chords A Teardrop And A Bottle Of Beer" 113
"Tryin' To Fall" 115
"Unhappy Day" 117
"Unnamed" 118
"Wars! Wars!" 119
"We Need A Home" 121
"Weeping" 122
"What Am I Going To Do" 123
"Willow Winds" 124
"Your Wedding Day" 125

Dedication

Volume #2 of Poems – Songs and Letters by "Vance"
is dedicated with the same respect, and thoughts, of
volume #1. that would be, to all the people who
played a part in providing me with a topic to write about,
or gave me a reason to write. their names are very
important to me, but need not be disclosed. they will
know who they are, if or when they read it.

A Special Dedication

**Volume #2 of Poems – Songs and Letters by "Vance,"
{entitled}
"The Awesome Oak"**
holds a very special meaning within. A referencing of
beauty, stature, and a growing love for that which should
never die, but last for ever.
It was one of my sister Roberta's favorite poems. She also
suggested it for the title of this volume. And so with that
same referencing of beauty, stature, and love, I dedicate this,
"The Awesome Oak" volume, of Poems – Songs and Letters
as follows.
To my older sister Roberta, my younger brother Larry,
my first cousin Jimmy Stoneking, my first cousin
Silas Allen, my brother-in-law Bob Martin, and another brother-
In-law's brother, Thomas Rogers. All of which have passed on
within a three month period prior to the publication of this book.
It has been a very heartfelt time for all the people whose lives
they touched, and meant so much to.
May you rest in peace and know that you are missed and loved.

Major Players

There is only one major player for this volume, and that would be my "wonderfully beautiful niece",
Tina Shay Rogers – Malloy.

This volume of Poems – Songs and Letters by "Vance" is titled, "The Awesome Oak." It was only made possible through the technological and literary talents provided by Tina.
Thank you very much!!!
Love you girl:

UNITED STATES MILITARY FORCES

I would also like to express my thanks and appreciation to the very brave and dedicated soldiers that make up all branches of this great country's military forces. Thank you for the protection and security you have provided for us all down through the years. I know that I speak for many more than myself when I say, we sleep much better at night knowing you are there to protect us.

THE WOUNDED WARRIORS!!!

100% of the proceeds or profits from this, "The Awesome Oak," volume #2 of poems songs and letters by Vance will be donated to the "Wounded Warrior Program."

{A personal note}
Thank you for all you have done, and the sacrifices you have made to allow me to live the good life and keeping me safe while doing so.
I can not thank you enough.
Indebtedly yours, Keith Vance!!!

Introduction

The poems songs and letters described and written in this, the Awesome Oak volume by Vance, refer to people, places, or events, either experienced by or known to the author. All accountings are true. Some, however, may be blessed with flavor, and color, or flair, if you will. Those will be left to the individual readers interpretation or discretion. There has been no intent to mislead or wrongly inform during the assembling of this volume.

Please keep in mind, a writer cannot squash that which flows from mind to paper. Neither imagination or integrity will permit.

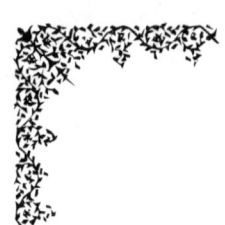

"The Awesome Oak"

this mighty oak was my favorite tree
through many hot days it shaded me

when I was told that it must fall
'twas a very sad day as I recall

I conquered my feelings, cut it and cried
left feeling abandoned, and empty inside

what a "Great Tree," it should have never died
perfect in stature, spread 54 inches side to side

the pain I felt showed clearly in my eyes
that same graceless feeling experienced by the sky

never shall another come with such visual embrace
more than 100 years it stood in this same place

a lost and lonely look lingered long upon my face
in the background I see the sky has fell from grace!!!
"What – A – Tree"

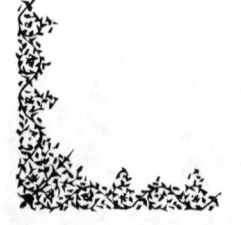

"AAAAAAAAH!!!"

at 4 AM

how many love's must I expose
to seek out pain that truly grows

the loves with lack of substance bear
the hurt that two hearts really share

why must I write of these events
with passion of the souls torment

a tornado ripping through my mind
like a tape recorder on rewind

brings visual to what's lost in time
holds anguish of a tortured kind

could it be for fear I can't sustain
that which mesmerized my brain

so strongly I must search my past
grasping for a love that lasts

what shall I do when memory leaves
and becomes furled into make-believe

imagination of untruthful things
cept with my love's, this cannot bring

heartfelt and kindred thoughts of yore
with truthfulness, I must implore

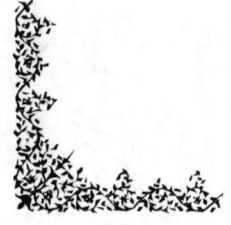

[AAAAAAAH continued]

my only hope is that I live
long enough to merit give

to all of that which I have written
birthed by truth to not be smitten

lest my life would be for naught
as love endeavors be my lot

for one who doubts should read the pages
discolored and dated through the ages

if they with this are still unsure
interview the ones procured!!!

"A Wanderers Heart"

you're a darling, you're an angel
you are everything most men need

but I'm just not like most men
and sweetheart, I never will be

ow it's too late for changes
they happen too damn slow

by the time you make one
it'll be time for me to go

I never look for an opening
I always make my own way

hearts are made to be broken
when naivety is in play

enjoy the contentment of playing the part
for you'll never possess, a wanderers heart!!!

{Excerpt from volume 1}

my weakness is women, they do strange things to me
though they're all the same, each one is different you see
my only trouble is, I love them all the same way
when my weakness set in, it came to stay
to be true to one, it could never ever be
always on the run, it's the weakness in me
please don't hold it against me, for what I've said and done
because I know when you're smiling, my hearts having fun!!!

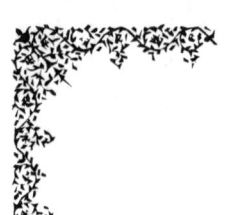

"All The Way Down"

[song]
well I've been down the road
sometimes I think too much

and there have been a few times
life tried to call my bluff

now I'm looking back
and I think I've had enough

I guess I had to get all the way down
before I could get back up

aw----listen to me mama-- you better hear
yeah hear--- what your daddy say
and if you don't like it baby--- spread your wings
honey--- an-d just fly away

well there has been a time or two
when the going--- got rough

and you were right beside me
just to help me do my stuff

I know you want my lovin'
so you gotta fill up my cup

I'm headed back down honey
so you can help me get back up

[All the way down continued]

aw---an overdose of lovin'----baby—O-D all over me
now if you don't want to mama--why the hell---
don't you just let me be
oh---the two of us to gather--sometimes
seems like luck
we fell into a spider web---messed around
and got stuck
well if you're my lucky charm
honey---you better---tighten up
you know that your daddy is all the way down
and you got-ta help him---get back up
(aw---get me up mama)

yeah---change the web your weavin'
don't be talkin' about leavin'

let me know you'll---stick around
put my feet back on the ground

cause the way things are going
"God"---knows I've had enough

yes I was---all away down
but now I'm gettin' back up

getting' up---mama---yeah---getting' up
with you
get down—up—up--down
get me up baby
just like you always do
(aw--- get me up mama)

"An Unfamiliar Place"

{for D. D'r}

my heart has found an unfamiliar place
seems everywhere I look I see your face

it tells my mind, I'm not sure what to do
I guess it's true, I may never get over you

the moonlight reminders of what we had
birth uninvited nightmares to leave me sad

when you were here, you ruled my soul
without you I'm lonely, I have no control

a rhyme without reason soon comes to an end
a love story glooms from the loss of a friend

if I hadn't known you before we fell in love
I would not feel empty from the lack there-of

The trust and presence that made life complete
as friends became lovers, and suffer defeat!!!

"Bad Habits"

(an unorthodox sonnet)

(for Kathy)

I've got all the bad habits, like cigarettes,
gambling, whiskey, women, and song

I guess between here and my early childhood
somehow I went a little bit wrong

With me around, it's often been said
the devil'd be better off dead

but don't let that fool you
I'll not try to rule you

cause simply, I am what I am
most time's, I just don't give a damn

the dying is easy and the living is hard
and the loving sometimes harder still

but you are the light of my life
I love you, and I always will!!!

"Bottle Bravery"

when I woke up I must've looked a mess
what really happened is anybody's guess
I suppose my mouth overloaded my ass
I said something they couldn't let pass
I reeked of clorox, puke, and tobacco spit
and I know damn well I didn't fall in it
so I guess what happened is plain to see
some thin-skinned smartass, scrubbed the floor with me
either that or they couldn't find a mop
after one of those insults I let drop
I kinda remember this one guy about the size of a mountain
I offered him a drink, he refused, and I started mouthin'
that "ole" bottle bravery brought on verbal abuse
a friend tried to turn it off, but it weren't no use
with boilermakers of Jim beam a runnin' through my veins
I could feel it creeping up my spine, and into my brain
I offered him a straight shot of my right hand
and he wound me up like a rubber band
either I hit the floor or the floor hit me
chairs and tables were flyin' and I couldn't see
I never knew a table leg could hurt so bad
when it was over I was really glad
for the loss of memory 100 proof gave me
what was coming next I didn't want to see
but it was a cleanest floor I have ever seen
and I'm wearing it well, courtesy of "ole" Jim Beam!!!

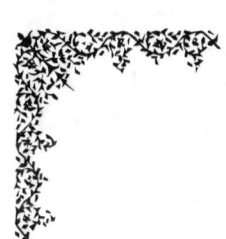

"Charade"

with this charade life handed me
should I invoke a guilty plea

or should I ride the winds of time
and pray they yield the perfect rhyme

will there come a time I can't endure
I think not, of one thing I am sure

my love for life I shall embrace
and always enhancement chase

have I not paid the price supreme
the loves I've lost are now in dreams

do I pay now for sins I've made
or conjured sins in my charade

from families I could not control
now serves struggle in my soul!!!

"Cryin' Eyes"

[song]
(for M.L.G.)
eyes – why don't you stop that cra-zy crying
you know it won't help anymore

my dar--lings gone away and left me
and it'll nev--er be like--it was before

so eyes – please stop – that crazy crying
for now – – it only makes it worse

you – know that – every tear drop fal – ling
comes – from a mem – ory of her

(talk this part)
you once saw things very clear
through the brighter side of life
never were you forced to face
all this trouble and strife
but then you had reasons
to be cheerful and shine on
not knowing one day you'd look
and find your real love gone
you were so busy being happy
you had no time to cry
that's when it happened
and you just wondered why

so now please stop that crazy crying
your turn--ing my whole world black

[Cryin' eyes continued]

you've cri—ed en--ough to flood the state of Texas
but it---will never---never ever---bring her back
[music run]
eyes---you must stop that crazy crying
I—know---it's so very hard to do
my hea--rt hurts e--nough as it is
and I don't need---any hel--p from you
no--- I don't need--- I don't need
any h—e—l—p fr—om---you--!!!

"Dirty Kerosene"

[song]
{chorus}

well I dipped my wick in dirty kerosene
and my lamp won't light at all
yes I dipped my wick in dirty kerosene
and I got all my lights cut off

now Mama says--she don't love me anymore
and our baby was born today
I said, pretty miss---there ain't no reason to be sore
how come you're-a-actin' this-a-way
she said, you dipped your wick in dirty kerosene
and that's enough for a start
you dipped your wick in dirty kerosene
and I ain't gonna be livin' in the dark
well the longer I live the less I learn
my lamp won't light and my fire won't burn
my woman don't love me---the little baby
thinks I mean
all because of that dirty kerosene
[end with chorus]
oh---I dipped my wick in dirty kerosene
and my lamp won't light at all
yes---I dipped my wick in dirty kerosene
and got all my lights cut off!!!

This song was actually written for a friend that was getting ready to go on a camping trip. While making his inspection and pre-trip of the necessary equipment, he found it impossible to light the lamps or heaters. His verbal assessment was that either the kerosene was too old or dirty, or the wicks were dirty, therefore, it would not permit the lamps to light. Hence the title, "Dirty Kerosene." Totally as innocent as the state of mind:

"Empty Promises And Lonesome Lies"

[song]

everything is different since you went away
I've been looking for you honey every night and day
dog-gone lonesome and low-down blue
ain't missing nothing but little "ole" you
come on back and see me
don't ya leave me alone
you know you're the one
that makes this house a home
listen to me baby
I'll do anything you say
just tell me that you are
coming back to stay
draw me a line
I won't cross it anymore
cause when you left the last time
it made my heart too sore
now I'm begging you honey
you got me on my knees
you know you're the one
that makes my life complete
if you don't come back
I don't know what I'll do
my life ain't nothing without you
call me up and tell me you'll be back to stay
and make these dog-gone blues go away
I'll pick you up at the airport in my private jet
or your own stretch limo – you ain't heard

[Empty promises and lonesome lies continued]

nothing yet
if you'd come back to me, we might go to
the moon
they're selling tickets now, why don't you
get here soon
buy a summer home up in Nantucket
it's nice and fancy, I know you'd love it
oh, by the way, before I let you go
did I mention, that I-I won the lotto
I'm not making it up, and there's no disguise
I'm just say--ing baby, you might be my demise
but if it all comes true you're gonna be surprised
about my empty promises and lonesome lies!!!

"Every Road I Take"

[song]

every roa---d I take – leads me to your house
and every tur---n I make – turns me to you

thought one--day soon I'd be ab--le to forget
and doing so – would help me face the truth

but I see now---that can never be
for you go---t the only thing – that controls me
yes you---'ve got the heart that beats in--side of me

that's why every roa---d I take – leads to your house
and every tur---n I make – turns me to you

my love for you's too strong – I'm not able to move on
and when I tr---y – thinking about you is all I can do

last night I drove around till I was haggard
just thinking of the way it was before

and I passed a house--I had been to many times
I can't believe I'm not welcome there-anymore

It's so hard to go home
for another night alone

those walls keep closing in--around my bones
I'm in a casket in--a world I've never known

now I know I'll never find
someone to ease my mind

[Every road I take continued]

fa--te has sealed my destiny
and my heart won't set me free

and my mind won't let me be
a kill---ing mem-ory is all I see

cause every roa---d I take – leads me to your house
and every tur---n I make – turns me to you

yes every roa---d I take – leads me to your house
and it hurts to know that I can't be there too!!!

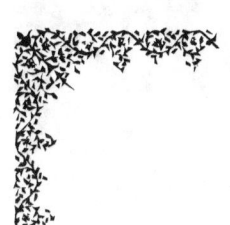

"For A Mother's Love"

(for Whitney's daughter)

oh I'd like to go swimming with mother
though it's not what it seems to be

he had to go quick, because she was sick
with a fear of upsetting me

yes I need to go swimming with mother
for we both loved the water you see

without her at home, I'm left all alone
and I can't put my mind at ease

so I will go swimming with mother
and dre--am of the ocean breeze

the smell of the air, the wind in my hair
gives contentment to final release

oh it's so nice to be swimming with Mama
for I know, that she will watch over me!!!

"For Destiny"

my father was in prison
and my mother lied to me

some say that's the reason
they named me Destiny

not really sure of family
and searching for identity

without a sense of being
there is no honor in my name

what difference would it make
if I turned out the same

oh my destiny, what could it be
am I lost so young and lonely

Lord, is this the way it should be
when your name is Destiny???

"Forty – Forty"

[song]

{chorus}
well – Lordy Lordy Lordy
here I am at 40-40
nd I don't have a damn thing to do
I gotta find me something quick
or I think I'm gonna be sick
I must be coming down with the blues

oh it's 40-40 Fairfax
damn – I wish I had a sixpack
and if I had a sixpack
I don't think I'd make it back
to the city
cause the way I feel today
with a little help to go astray
I might go grab my baby
by the – – – –
oh – give me some – rocking chair or granddad
I think I'm gonna break bad
I know there's a lot that we can do
I gotta find my baby quick
she's a popsicle on a stick
and she's got the on – ly cure for these blues
yes my baby is a lady
and she never tells me maybe
she kno – ws exact – ly what she ne – eds to do

{chorus}
well – Lordy Lordy Lordy
here I am at 40-40

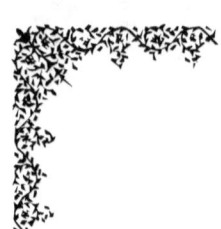

[Forty – forty continued]

and I don't have a damn thing to do
I gotta find me something quick
or I think I'm gonna be sick
I must be coming down with the blues
oh Lordy Lordy Lordy
here I am at 40-40
doing everything I've always loved to do

Rock 'n Rol – Koochie –Koo
and that good "ole" Boo – ga – loo
maybe try a little tutti-frutti too
Lordy – Lordy – Lordy---40-40
heah now!!!
That's the only cure for these blues!!!

"Happy Tears"

(to life's pleasures)
I do not weep for a love that didn't last
or for things that went wrong in my past

my tears are for the joy, they are my happy tears
for the love bestowed on me throughout the years

o good will come, from crying for years gone by
you are left with memories, not to question why

I have no time to waste in the winter of my life
I have only left to say, I always loved my wife

with much happiness in those few years we had
it would serve it all unjust, if I were to be sad

the many countless times I've enjoyed happiness
bears witness to how much I truly have been blessed

and so as my time grows shorter, in these snowy years
though I may weep, these tears, are happy tears!!!

"Happy With What I've Got"

[song]

well there's a whole lot wrong with what I've got
and nothing wrong with what I had
I never wanted anything that wasn't good
and never took anything that was bad
always tried---to face life with a smile
cause I don't look good with a frown
so I think I'll take another trip around the world
before I lay my body down
[repeat]
yeah, I'm gonna take it 'round the world one more time
and then I'll lay my body down

I guess I've had about everything I wanted
except a million dollars and a yacht
and I know I could have handled that
although it might have got me in a spot
we all have our own way of telling
if we're happy with the love we've found
but we probably wouldn't know the difference
if the real thing came around
so I'll keep what I've go--t and stay happy
until I lay my body down

yeah I'll take it around the world--one more time
and then I'll lay my body down
while I'm making that trip
I'm gonna try to remember
all the good love I have found
I'm gonna hold on tight an stay happy
cause I don't look good with a frown
yeah I'll take it round the world—one more time
then I'll lay my body down!!!

"Hey George"

hey George, how you doing today
I thought I'd drop by, to see what ya had to say

thought maybe we might talk a little bit about old times
even have a drink or two, to keep from losing our minds

'll tell you my problems, then you can tell me yours
though they're both almost over, just from times course

all my problems make up the titles of your songs
I guess that means, I must-a-done something wrong

you know George, it's good to be able to talk to you
I've had so many heartaches, that your songs got me through

sometimes I feel we're so close our life was poured from the same bottle
it was labeled, hell – bent – for – heartache, with a wide open throttle

I really think I know you George, although we've never met
I could've written you a song, that no-one would forget

so if it's all right with you, I'll tell my story first
and hope that I get through, before we die of thirst

("quoth the master")

I stopped loving her today, aw-but she thinks I still care
I bet she's looking at a picture of me, without her there

(Hey George continued)

and if drinking don't kill me, I might make it to the door
now she was my rock, until I took that grand tour

oh I'm still doing time, in a place with no light
and I still make believe, that I'm ragged, but I'm right

now the bottle's on the table
and I'll drink till I'm not able

cause these days I barely get by
is it the life I live, or, why baby why

oh she made blue, the color of the blues
and you know George, no one can feel your shoes

it's your turn George, then I'll get on out-a-here
and if we're real lucky, we won't run out of beer

but that's okay, I'll send my baby on a beer run
cause what my woman can't do, can't be done
"See you on the flip Possum"!!!

"I Cry"

I cry for sadness
I cry for fear

I cry for loss of life
I cry because I'm wear

I cry for people who are lost
I cry for those who paid the cost

I cry for those who don't believe
I cry for those who can't conceive

I cry for those who will not see
I cry for what can never be

I cry for peace I cry for war
I cry for what we had before

I cry that we may all survive
I cry for nail--scarred hands that tried!!!

"If You Still Love Me Then"

[song]
you pro-mised you would never leave me
but today--- I find myself alone

though you did-n't mean to deceive me
it still hur--ts the same, once it's done

hon---ey there will come a time someday I know
you'll remember how I begged you not to go

[chorus]
and if you still love me then
come on back where you've been
you know that I'll still love you
with a love that's true
so if you still love me then
come on back where you've been
we can work it out I know
because I love you so
and if you still love me then
we'll go places we've never been
but only if, you still love me then

the memory of your love--li-ness
causes me so much pain

nothing can erase the lone--liness
th---at missing---you brings

I hope you'll see you had all you nee-ded
when you felt so uncomple--ted
[end with chorus]

[If you still love me then continued]

and if you still love me then
come on back where you've been
you know I still love you, with a love that's true
so if you still love me then, come on back where you've been
we can work it out I know, because I love you so
and if you still love me then, we'll go places we've never been
but only if, you still love me then!!!

"I'll Sing You A Letter"

I'll sing you a letter
cause I do that better
than I write, while I'm driving along

through the top of the trees
words fall from the breeze
to find their place in my song

darling it's been two days
and I'm counting the ways
I will love you upon my returning

well two days is too long
but your love keeps me strong
to be in your arms is my yearning

just one more full day
on our towels we'll lay
and make love to the ocean's roar

I'll dream of the time
you will be forever mine
and I'll leave your arms nevermore!!!

"In Memory Of"

this is for all the ones whom I need not mention
from 1965 to 1990, like me, they needed attention

each and everyone, like me, had feelings and desires
and were victims of a love that had recently expired

we cried and shared our stories while we held each other tight
we cradled the kind of love that gets you through the night

I pray that I was good for them, by playing out my part
each name remains embedded, deep inside my heart

I beckon them to serve me now as in my youth
with warm memories to help me hide the truth

with many thanks I greet thee where I dwell
to recall a time when hearts were young and frail

all of my life's seasons have duly served their cause
and so to you, with open arms, I will take my pause
thank you all!!!

"Justice"

(to me)
I have no reason to convey, the pain and hurt I feel today
truth be told I'm not in play, 'tis forlorn love held in dismay

oh my "God", to compare
the love and happiness i've shared

from lives in turmoil to a love that would forever last
and now with much regret, prophecy, becomes my past

at one time I was told but would not listen
otherwise my heart would glisten

there will be a holder of the key, when consolation doth appear
un-mask, no harm will come, the price of love is very clear

one holds the heart and soul of many
but his own heart and soul are empty

true love escapes him through his life
his just reward is full-blown strife

oh maker of dreams from whence I come
is there no reverence for what I've done

for these indiscretion's, can I not atone
or should I be left with envy of alone

because alone I'll never be, I'm the holder of a memory
for all the hearts I've warmed and washed with ecstasy

I can only hope the ones I have abused, in the end can laugh
for they shall write, my epitaph!!!

"Kathleen, My Kathleen"

(to my soul-mate)
oh Kathleen, my Kathleen
if only I could have seen
how much to my life you would mean

oh Kathleen, my Kathleen
if I would have had a way of knowing
how much for you my love was growing

oh Kathleen, my Kathleen
young loves fever cannot compare
to feelings found in mirrors of empty stares

oh Kathleen, my Kathleen
if I could just have known
I know I would have been shown
life's course to cease heart grieving
to be more comforting than leaving

oh Kathleen, my Kathleen
ye be the one I chose to marry
our memories through life I carry

oh Kathleen, my Kathleen
while lonely sadness brings life's winter
alive are memory's of springs splendor

oh Kathleen, my Kathleen
your love still lives to bring me life
in memory when you were my wife

[Kathleen, my kathleen continued]

oh Kathleen, my Kathleen
you know I'll never say goodbye
I'll hold you through the day I die
as my body fails and life does slip
your name be last, to cross my lips

oh Kathleen, my Kathleen
such a beautiful name, it holds a dream
this dream I shared, with my Kathleen!!!

"Lay Your Lovin' Down"

[song]
I've been waiting for tonight ever since you left
now it's finally here and I can't help myself

[chorus]
lay your Lovin' down-- spread it all around
baby hear my plea and put the hurt on me
you know you got to-- lay your Lovin' down
the fever is raging from my head to my toe
a little voice inside sayin' go-go-go
lay your Lovin' down eu-- spread it all around
aw baby hear my plea and put the hurt on me
you know you've got to lay your Lovin' down

you know I've been suffering since you went away
so before you go again you're gonna hear me say

lay your Lovin' down--make some Lovin' sounds
you know I can't wait-- so before you vacate
you better lay your Lovin' down

[Lay your lovin' down continued]

now it's a right time to tell you that I'm glad you're back
and if you don't make a move I'm about to attack
so "ba—by", lay your Lovin down, eu-- you've got the best around
now if you don't pursue I'm gonna come unglued
so lay your Lovin' down, lay your Lovin' down
em-m ba—by, spread it all around-- make those lov—in' sounds
oh, baby-- hear my plea and put the hurt on me
you know you've got to lay your Lovin' down
yeah, spread it on real thick now, aw—make it happen quick now
you're like jelly on bread-- hear what I said
e—m-m-mmm--eu----e- put the hurt on me
ba—a--by
Lay—Your--Lovin'--Down!!!

(beginning nine lines from the bottom use different voice tones, preferably, from gruffy to gravel base with modulation at the appropriate places. Use a lover's influenced tone on the last line.)

"Life's Perfect Rhyme"

(dismantling disaster)

what comes from within the mind
are the perils of all time
the pain, unhappiness, and discontent
leaves us warped and sometimes bent
so badly that we can not gather
all the thoughts that really matter
the mind gives way to idle chatter
with end results that will but shatter
the hopes and dreams of family
friends and loved ones disbelieve
the truth is just so hard to bear
for all the ones that really care
can there not be another way
eternity could have its say
than put the hearts involved on play
with feelings left in disarray
oh, if I could turn back time
to put all lives in perfect rhyme
'twould be a goal I'd hold in store
for lives of happiness I would implore
no more to hurt the ones we love
but comfort those we're thinking of
the end could be a perfect time
if mind allows a perfect rhyme

*****

(written for an old friend the day after his demise)
He had been leaning towards forgetfulness
He chose his own resolve

"Life's Levy"

I can't leave drinking behind
I do it till I'm out of my mind

for the memories that won't let me be
of all the loves that won't set me free

in a life that does not know remorse
leaves nothing to chance at the source

I expect nothing but what I am due
I shall die with good memory's of you

I have no desire for seeking release
from a pain unwilling to cease

instead, my heart opens wide
with nothing left inside to hide

life's best was offered and conceived
and mine returned somewhat bereaved

there is no way I would deny
life gives to all if we but try

the emptiness one feels from alone
we receive in gifts life has shown

be it prosperity, position, opportunities, or romance
of life's fruits, we have not eaten by chance

[Life's levy continued]

as lovers of life we are always choosing
knowing full well the chances of losing

taking mostly what we want only
left--with Life's Levy of Lonely!!!

"Long Way To Dover"

[song]
well it's a long drive up to Dover this morning
but not long enough to get over you

yes it's a long-long drive to Dover today
as I mix our memory's with the dew

and as the Highway goes on
I see what we wanted today

but last night we were blinded by anger
and said things we didn't mean to say

and now it's such a long drive to Dover
but not long enough to get over you

with every mile I rehash our disagreements
then compare them to the love we once knew

as the milestones go by I can count my mistakes
although it may be a little too late

my darling, I hope happiness finds you
for you've had much too long to wait

now it's a long--long way to Dover this morning
but not long enough to drive my heartaches away

this "ole" bridge across the Bay
is so much longer today

wish I could build one from my heart to yours
but I'll never have the chance, I know that it's over

[Long way to dover contiuned]

I gave you more pain than your heart could endure
so I'll say my goodbyes on my way home from Dover

a little wish for you, as life you go through
and a heart filled with love that is yours

I'm sorry for the pain and tears, I've brought you
and I hope you never--have to cry anymore!!!

"Look At Me"

look at me honey, and tell me the truth
are you sure this is what you want to do

in my life there is only one way
that's the way you go if you stay

you will be happy when we're having fun
but what will you do when the fun is done

I may leave tomorrow and come back again
I change directions just like the wind

when I leave it's not for putting you down
I'll love you the same when I come back around

I was born with excitement for another game
if I return, will you still fan my flame

so before you decide make sure what you see
sweetheart, is this really where you want to be???

"Lost In Time"

oh it seems I'm lost in time
always searching for a rhyme

like Shakespeare without a sonnet
or a maiden with no bonnet

I have only left to try life's meaning
then maybe find a new beginning

shall there be solace in my answer
or is this loss, a cureless cancer

I search but find no happiness
still with no answer I possess

the broken'st of broken hearts
with every break I played the part

Oh, have I lost the reason in the rhyme
or am I truly, lost in time???

"Love"

(for Ruth)
love is like a fruit
that grows on a tree

sometimes the limbs are full
while other times they are free

when real love is in season
it will not tarry without reason

one must feel the fullness of
set path towards a lasting love

both working for same feelings
will produce loves full yielding

true love cannot be found by asking
a worthwhile love is very tasking

I fall in love most every day
only to watch it slip away

through reasons of immaturity
I have no offering of security

while in the springtime of my life
I should not be looking for a wife

with practice if I work enough
and build resistance to a bluff

through recognition of what's real
may someday bring a true love deal

[Love continued]

love can be nice when you're together
due diligence prevents stormy weather

although so quiet you may be
your eyes portray a love for me

true to silence you remain
I feel your interest and proclaim

in this same way you do for me
your love I feel but cannot see

if proven blind I would truly know
this love of ours would surely grow

oh 'tis this kind of love I seek
where neither party needs to speak

from just a feeling one would know
that which sets a lovers heart aglow

where questions are unnecessary
and eye to eye reveals a sharing

this kind of love's not mine by rhyme
but this kind of love, is for all time!!!

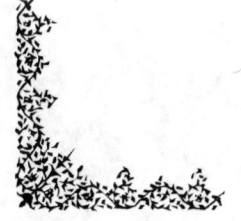

"Loves Weakest Link"

{for Margie}
it's not that you don't love me
instead, 'tis my love that is gone

I was never one for misery
so I'll just be moving on

you will think back and realize
as I have done before

a spark stays hot but to disguise
the flame that burns no more

to another, someday you will say
much like I have said to you

as they desire your pleasing way
but your love cannot be true

then I, in a yester memory, make you think
in our chain of love, mine was the weakest link!!!

"Midnight Memory"

there's a problem on the horizon
no one can feel it but me
yes there's a problem, and I've tried to disguise it
but darling, it won't let me be
blue Mondays have never been problems
I can survive the weeks misery
but it's Friday, and Saturday's coming
and the weekends just petrify me
oh, there's nothing so scary, as the solid cold silence
with the haunting and taunting of memory's we made
appearing in dream form to tell me
your absence is the price I must pay
from Friday at midnight I'm praying for Monday
cause I'm all alone, with your memory
("oh it's midnight, with your memory")
on Fridays you seem very special
and it cuts through my sleep like a knife
then on Saturday you show me just how close
you came to being my wife
on Sunday my dream world starts fading
with an Angel – like form at my door
I'm awakened by an image of you
walking out of my life evermore
well I'm okay from Monday through Friday
you try hard to reinsure me

[Midnight memory continued]

but I remember the one time you left dear
and the hurt just won't let me be
are you really working, how can I be sure
the trust I once had is gone
and the mental misery I bring on myself
for the weekends, goes on – and – on
so it seems fate has decided, no choice left for me
I'll be praying for Monday from Friday at midnight
all alone with your memory

("oh it's midnight, for eter-ni-ty !!!")

"The Midnight Mumbler"

it's the morning after the end of the world
nothing seems very real

as I go driving by it seems like I'm high
and the shock just can't be concealed

on the side of the highway I see a picture of you
as I head down the road, oh – no

your face on a road sign, but I think your still mine
and I know that just can't be so

the tallest of high-rises cannot match in my eyes
the beauty that you hold in store

my second glanced billboard is captioned with
why now, and what for? As your picture emerges once more

always, the morning after the end of the world
when nothing seems very real

while driving by, I know that I'm high
from the unhealthy feelings I feel

oh I don't know, or can't say, why I feel this way
it don't seem like a natural thing

but if the end of the world is anything like this
I would prefer a seesaw to a swing

[The midnight mumbler continued]

Or, maybe a yo-yo
but woah-woah
the world won't go
this time we're moving too slow
rock – a – bye back and forth
here we go once more
lightning just struck
guess I'm out of luck
hung around and got burned
will I never learn?
Oh – no, the world won't turn
someday you might say
when you start to play
every way any day
roll on muddy river, you sure make me quiver
and shiver whenever you say
oh – no it's too slow
and I know it won't go
I look down the highway see a picture of you
but I know, oh I know, it's not true
your face is a road sign
because you were never mine
so woah-woah
the world won't go
I learned, got burned
the world won't turn
oh-no, it's too slow
oh-no, it won't go
one step at a time, gee-whiz you feel fine
you look good
you know that you do
so cute, yeah so cute
it's around and around

[The midnight mumbler continued]

some up an some down
some up in the air, some under the ground
it won't turn – got burned
so slow – can't go
oh no
your face on a road sign
tells me you're not mine
oh no – oh no
now the dogs meowing
and the old cat is growling
in the bird that said bye-bye
to a rat that says why why
then a Mockingbird's my-my
tells me you lie-lie again
oh the spring of the year
must surely be here
and I wonder where it has been
cause this snow is so deep
I can't hardly sleep
and I sure wish that I had a friend
I might freeze to death
when I can't get my breath
sometimes it feels like the end
I'd like to get out of here there's no doubt
but I must think clear to get out
oh, it's a lullaby play – time
a scrambled up brain time
an "ole" Hank Williams pain – time
tear – jerk – an – cry – cry
an old bedtime lullaby
sing me to sleep, would you try

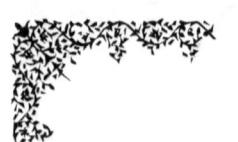

[The midnight mumbler continued]

for I – – I – – don't know
when I go – what I did know
an ocean of teardrops, a River of blood
could be the cause of an open heart flood
it's ever so painful you can't get rid of
then crying time starts
with the old bleeding hearts
oh I wonder why why
with a Mockingbird's my my
oh it's turning so slow
I don't think it'll go
the way you do, and you know
you're oh so – so hard to let go
you might say I can't learn, you might say I got burned
oh – my – why – why the world won't turn
mmm –mmm –daa –de –di
the morning after the end of the world
oh – my – why – why
a jumbled up – brain
causin' me such pain
memories of
much love
oh – my – why – why, oh – no
so – slow, love won't go
can't learn, got burned, aw it won't turn
pictures and road signs
diving boards and grapevines
to skinny dippin' good times
to white coats and lockdowns
oh it's the morning after the end of the world
and why – why is my – my world not around
it's a low down lonesome sound
and you are no – where, to be found!!!

"Missing You"

{for Kathleen, my wife}
missing you is the hardest thing I've ever had to do
compared to life's surprises, and I have had a few

the absence of having you for my very own
has introduced a timed resolve that I must be alone

when the longing for your better part has ceased
the desire to wander aimlessly becomes increased

knowing not and caring less what tomorrow brings
nothing, could repair my damaged heart strings

when claim to fame is to abide in a life of solitude
your consolation is a love with no feelings to include

eventually, the time comes feelings grow numb
but lingering pain tells the worst is yet to come

not having thee, to be without the one I love so true
missing you, is the hardest thing, I've ever had to do!!!

"Morbidity"

I wrote it, then I read it
still I can't believe I said it

words that holds so little meaning
could it be that I am leaning

toward an explanation not too sound
for all the puzzles I have found

never knowing what might be there
I could not see, why should I care

yet from within there comes a cry
you must divulge before you die

no foreign language or native tongue
could translate the wrongs I've done

now that I think clearly, nor shall I
instead, with morbidity, I will die!!!

"My Heart"

memory's need a heart like mine to cling to
and my heart needs memories to sing to

I prefer they be my own
but if a forlorn lover needs a home

my heart is always open wide
to comfort memory's from their side

my heart will never get so old
to shut a memory in the cold

it does one good to hold the hand
of sadness from another man

nor will my heart try to compare
the pain and sorrow living there

no two memories are the same
love is always, a situational game!!!

"My One True Love"

[for 3-28-60]

love don't leave these things we've made
for the first time I am afraid

I cannot emerge from loves strong current
instead I pray for a deterrent

one that pulls me far from danger
and leaves me with loss of anger

I want this not to be severe
for two hearts that have lived in fear

of being torn by distance between years
or misunderstanding of feelings clear

I pray only, those who know
will allow true feelings grow

and denounce the interference of
what has been my one true love!!!

"Never Alone"

I will never live my life alone
while paying for the things I've done

loneliness shall not infringe my space
life's luxuries and comforts will help me face

what comes my way without defeat
still emptiness remains in me

perhaps from a love I could not see
now I'm longing for it's company

though always trying to be aware
of any and all that may have cared

knowing my purpose in life is to make a lover feel
deserving of all pleasures from a love that's real

we are all alone if not for "God", and his loving son
He came as a companion, for the ones, who are alone!!!

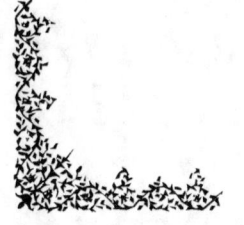

"No Desire To Lie To You"

if it takes lying and cheating to be first class
then I suppose that I will always be last

one thing I have no desire to do
would be to ever lie to you

though you have no problem with accusing
I have not been worthy of your abusing

should I have need to tell you more
my mind, my body, does implore

I would never judge you by things I've done
I believe you to be more honorable than this one

therefore I leave with one request
please let your heart be my guest

I promise I'll be true, and never bring you tears
happiness will flow, like a river through the years!!!

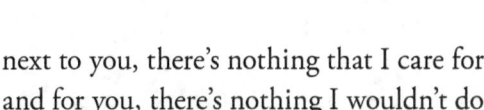

"Next To You"

next to you, there's nothing that I care for
and for you, there's nothing I wouldn't do

next to you, there is no-one that I dream of
yes I have you, but I'm no-one, next to you

my life now, has lost its meaning
only emptiness lives inside of me

I know that someday you'll be leaving
but I do not want to look at what I see

you have tried very hard to show me
it don't matter what I put you through

your forgiving love is overwhelming
and I know that I do not deserve you

you're a mountain high, I am but a valley
and I am no-one, next to you

should you tell me that you love me
of course I respond, I love you too

I can not survive in your world darling
our time for love has come and gone

it's like that one last rose of summer
where only lonely, lingers on

You hold all heavenly constellations
in ransom for the beauty you are due

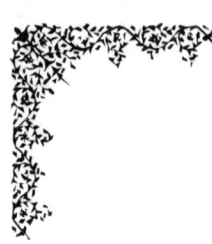

[Next to you continued]

You light my world as consolation
still I remain, no one next to you

you freely gave a love unending
with no expectations due of me

and with you each day a new beginning
but with me are dreams of being free

not one loves doubt, did you inquire
or impose the need my love to starve

for I was fueled by my own fire
a needed legacy still left to carve

my heart went places undiscovered
the high, much higher than the sky

to compete with you, I could not win
non-compete, will end by asking why

I can only come to one conclusion
as pleasuring you I love to do

we were meant for love, not confusion
I shall remain, still no-one, next to you!!!

"No More Tears Over You"

[song]
[chorus]
///*10 lines-- first four slow--- next six a little faster *\\\
there'll be no more tears over you dear
I'm all healed from the hurt that you caused
and they'll be no more heartaches to follow
for I've found a new path to walk
[this part of chorus a little faster]
no more misery'd moments
spent in sleepless nights
no more tears on my pillow
I've traded darkness for light
oh they'll be no more tears over you dear
for at last I have found a new life

nothing but good times am I headed for
so don't hold your breath till I knock on your door

there was a line to be drawn
and that line I just drew

I just told myself
no more tears over you

you live your life your way
and I'll do the same with my own

and I'll give you my word
that I'll leave you alone

now's the time to forget
and I know that I can

[No more tears over you continued]

for I'm getting better
I feel like a new man

(chorus – – both parts)
so they'll be no more tears over you dear
I'm all healed from the hurt that you caused
and they'll be no more heartaches to follow
for I've found a new path to walk
[chorus – – faster part]
no more misery'd moments
spent in sleepless nights
no more tears on my pillow
I've traded darkness for light
oh they'll be no more tears over you dear
for at last I have found a new life

so have lots of fun
and be happy all the time

for you can be sure
I'll be having mine

yeah, be proud of yourself
for what you can do

for you've seen the last time
I'm gonna cry over you

[end with faster part of chorus]
no more misery'd moments
spent in sleepless nights
no more tears on my pillow
I've traded darkness for light
no they'll be no more tears over you dear
for at last I have found a new life!!!

"No Remorse"

oh if I could but bend your ear
as you watch me shed a joy-tear
for blessings received through the years

the words are lost for "God's" great gifts
I no longer have need for the spiritual lifts
I have topped and watched the powers shift

if I were to only have one wish
'twd be that I not be remiss
to yester-loves of tenderness

'tis the things we know that mean the most
we must replace at any cost
so not to suffer a love that's lost

the painful harm our egos build
until the heart or mind wont yield
yet hides behind a phantom shield

oh tell me why I cannot say
thank you for the yesterdays
may "God" replace the love you gave

all memory's of my loves are good
though rearranged from whence they stood
they were changed to fit my mental good

when they're lining up is done
I shall say, "I had much fun."
and rank them all, as number one

[No remorse continued]

the part of your life you shared with me
is alive in instant memory
with all compared, true love agrees

you have all left me in appreciation
an unending love that held no ration
with pure displays of hungry passion

and now I've said it, with no remorse
life's final run, I've stayed the course
just to be guided by a true love source

the means no longer justify the end
in the long run the means are friends
if real love is there when you begin!!!

"The One That Got Away"

though my title fails her sorely
this lady fills that bill
I miss her so adoringly
her pleasures haunt me still
to quote the friends that envied me
"you should have imposed your will"
with respect for her desire of chastity
by her pleasured company I was thrilled
and so my memory's yield a glowing
while I watched her body sway
with complete content of knowing
as through my dreams we play
she no longer lives in haunting
for she's the one, that got away!!!

{Insert from volume 1}

"North Carolina – 1965"

oh the stars they glitter brightly as I look up through
the trees
the deep dark blue of nights psychic portrays a picture
that I see
the lonesome call of the cricket conversing with a
frog
the night winds carry a ringing echo of a far – off
barking dog
in the distance I can hear the traffic and the roar of
city life
cutting through the trees so silent to reassure my
plight
it was such a pretty picture, there goes a shooting
star
making its trip's across the heavens to sparkle near
and far
if I could but hold this magic, I would release my
dreams
for there is nothing quite so lovely, as heavens perfect
scene

"Ode To Olie James"

[song]
I'd love to go again to a revival in our town
when singing good old gospel music
would bring salvation down

I remember how my mother would dance with the
Holy Ghost
and speak in unknown tongues, with the Holy Lord
Of Hosts
there was preaching and praying unlike you've never
heard
but the biggest thrill of all was when Olie sang about
the bird
[music run, and in the background]
[the 1st verse of The Great Speckled Bird]

{next verse}
a revival has a lot of people, that don't understand
the spirit of "God"
but if they would try it they'd like it, and the path
they chose to trod
everybody starts shouting – bathing in heavenly fun
nobody wants to leave until the Holy Spirit is
done
they're all shaken hands and loving – no one seems the
same
and in the background you can hear the sounds of that
gentle man, named Olie James

[music run, and in the background]
[the 2nd verse of The Great Speckled Bird]

"Open-Ended"

so you think I'm lonely, but that can never be
I will never be lonely, as long as there is me

some say I'm in denial and will not face the truth
that I live in a fantasy along with dreams of youth

fantasy and dreams are a nano-second apart
one must possess both to have a full heart

allow fantasy and dreams to change destiny
then you will watch life give birth to reality

a dream allows our imagination to run wild
in fantasy we imagine this with visual style

you imagine your world and see it through
that's what dreams and fantasy help you do

my world is exactly, what I see it to be
and loneliness, shall never captivate me!!!

"Poetry's Bleeding Hearts"

5 AM from my bed
how meaningless the end may seem
'tis truly that of a poet's dream

my work sometimes I think does show
with deaths order, how it reeks of Poe

while other pieces live in fear
of unassembled rhymes so clear

the influence holds a healthy sound
between them both will go around

one could write forever without pause
continuously searching for his cause

filled with happy endings by one's hand
yet the suffering soul of the other man

one world could not hold them at same time
opposites, within the confines of the mind

Williams life seemed filled with joy
with constant searching for employ

to achieve submission of another's spouse
perhaps inspired him then to write about

the heart-ache of a deed like this
would sure be absent of the bliss

'twas then that he was at his best
the gifted one achieved his quest

[Poetry's bleeding hearts continued]

from start to finish keeps one's attention
most times he lost, as he would mention

to create a scene you cannot win
brings mental torture at the end

then there was Edgar, and we all know
not one could touch our Mr. Poe

he lived in misery, he lived in fright
and wrote it down without delight

his life was short, his heart was sore
he let us know, down by the shore

he loved, he lost, and he paid the cost
but what we gained, from what he lost

not one other can compare
to attempt would be unfair

with him unhappiness filled the air
but all he wrote held so much flair

Shakespeare and Poe gave heart felt work to last
forever
leaving us in awe and searching for a line so
clever

how clear it is, they were to be
the bleeding hearts, of poetry!!!

"Rainbow"

[song] [chorus]
rainbow – rainbow where did you go
oh where did you go, oh where did you go
rainbow – rainbow where did you go
you took my baby and I miss her so
rainbow – rainbow – you went away
and you went to stay
you took my baby away

you came with the sunshine and the rain
my darling was there too
with her pretty eyes of blue
then you flashed your colors
as though for to say
I'm taking your baby away
oh rainbow – rain-bow
where did you go, oh where did you go
you took my baby and I miss her so
rainbow – rainbow, oh where could you be
come back and bring my baby back to me

ever since she's been gone
everything is wrong
only you know what I lack
won't you please bring her back
without her you see
life is total misery
oh rainbow bring my baby back to me

[end with chorus]

"Reaching Out"

I called on the Gaither's, Jason Crabb, and Penrod too
I even called Billy Graham, just to see what he could do
I reached out to the Isaacs, Ivan Parker, and the great George Beverly Shea
I listened to the Oak Ridge boys, and the Happy Goodman family, to see if they knew the way
I saw the tears of Jimmy Swaggart, watched Franklin Jensen drop one or two
they kinda looked like me, cause I have dropped a few
had a crying time with Joel Olstein, pastor Prince and TD Jake's
Prince and Olstein got me ready, and Jake's gave me the shakes
Jakes's job was different, he broke me down and showed my shame
he'd show you the hell you're living in, then pull you from the flame
Bishop Jakes woke me one morning, I guess about five, to help me see
he said, "get out of bed and read your Bible, you know where you should be
how long will you go on acting like you have never heard
the calling that is laid on you, is written in "God's" Holy Word!!!

"Red Vette Blues"

{song}
well keep on rolling baby, roll on out a here
yeah I said keep on rolling baby, roll on out a here
ain't had this piece of mind
in damn near 20 years
so keep that Red Vette rollin'
and roll a—way all my tears
all right

now you are nothin' but trouble
I should-a left you alone
yeah baby you're trouble
should-a let you alone
but I was born for trouble honey
and trouble's always been my song
and I was roll—ing, rolling from that day on
[music run]

if I ever meet, another one like you
oh baby, if I meet anyone like you
I'm gonna pack my bags, hop a train
and honey I'll be rollin' too-- hey now
and I'll keep on rollin' mama
till that train runs out of track
yeah I'll keep a rollin' baby
till that "ole" train runs out-a-track
your daddy's gonna roll roll roll
And he ain't coming back

I got the Re--ed Ve—ette B-lues
lord I don't know what to do
I got them Red Vette blues
and sure don't know what to do

[Red Vette blues continued]

you put my mind in a bind, what is it all coming to
you're just comin' and goin', baby it's all the same
comin' and goin', ya know it's all the same
you got me in a situation
where I don't even know my name
hey hey

[Music run]

aw—ba--by take that pretty Red Vette
and don't you come around no more
listen to me honey, take your Vette
and baby don't you come round no more
you done it to me where it hurts
and my heart is too damn sore

I got them Red Vette Blues
baby it's all the same
just comin' and goin', you know it's all the same
ya done got me to a point, I don't even know my name
a-yodel-lay-hay-hee-hee-hee
I got the Re—ed Ve—tte B—lu-es
that's right
baby that's what I say, hey hey
these little Red Vette Blues
ain't never gonna go away
hey – hey

"Right The Wrongs"

she was a Bloomingdale's lady, shopping at Zayre
I could not imagine, what she was doing there

such an obvious misplacement, of one so fair
her eloquence and style, fragranced the air

I said, "my lady B, what are you doing at Z?"
She smiled as she looked, and replied to me.

"Life has been fun, life has been grand
but life does not always deal a good hand

as a matter of fact, it's because of a man
that you see me today, just as I am."

As she turned the corner, I knew she was gone
I wanted to catch her, but I knew it was wrong

she was a lady lost, where she did not belong
nothing I could say, would rewrite her song

• • •

she was a registered nurse, now a bartender
with dreams of yesterday, not hard to remember

her life was so good, she had everything
the ring of a phone, bad news would bring

no one has the right, to change dreams of another
unless, of course, if the caller is your lover

She had placed all her trust but her trust betrayed
and her dreams hinged on vows that were made

[Right the wrongs continued]

I tried to console, but her pain was too strong
I knew nothing I'd say, could right all the wrong

• • •

she was a schoolteacher, happy as could be
she now sleeps on the streets, in Washington DC

she prepared family meals, from her own kitchen
now begging for pennies, but she's not bitchin'

yes, she had a good life, but she threw it away
for cocaine at a party, on a boring day

as I tried to talk to her, she kept mumbling on
I knew nothing I'd say, could rewrite her song

• • •

a young college student, she loved sky diving
her favorite pastime was pranks, and conniving

so for what ever reason, the reasons she'd mix
in all walks of life, that's how she got her kicks

if you are a tempter of death, you will never succeed
you can lose everything, while fulfilling your needs

the dive was her last one, because she was bored
she had a parachute, but would not pull the cord

her diving companions all chased, but in vain
they could not change, what had been ordained

• • •

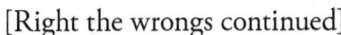

[Right the wrongs continued]

there she stands, a mother, all alone on a cliff
with a knife in her hand, just hoping she'll slip

it's been an unbearable day, let's take life away
and no one wants to hear, what she has to say

her life has been broken, from love just a token
through the reality of dreams, life has spoken

not one thing she planned, can be held in her hand
now the taker of life has command

as she cradles her children, and baby just born
in a world of make-believe she is torn

what happens, she leaps, with no one to keep
or to hold her, as she falls asleep!!!

• • •

he lived in a high-rise in Roslyn
at night he could see Washington

from his balcony, a beautiful sight
all peaceful and calm, with its lights

but that night he didn't notice the view
he was suffering from things no one knew

a bankrupt business put his family in shame
all chance was gone for clearing his name

the next morning's papers, would tell it all
how his trip through life, had caused his fall

• • •

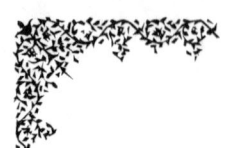

[Right the wrongs continued]

there she stands, at the window looking down
it's a 14 story flight, to the ground

she's an airline stewardess and used to such heights
but today something happened that just wasn't right

no one cares, and no one sees
as she drops down on her knees

Lord knows it's hard, to find a life desire
when others, keep putting out your fire

she stands up and looks toward the stars
and asked forgiveness for all her scars

she prays, "God"please be with me on my final flight
and guide me gently, through the night

• • •

there he sits, head bowed and alone
life turned his last page, he's on his own

feeling as though he'd lost his best friend
all lovers are gone and life's at an end

it had been many years since he left home
life's luring voice had enticed him to roam

it's twisted interpretation had not been fair
homeless and helpless with just a blank stare

he was finding it is so hard to live
for he had nothing left to give

[Right the wrongs continued]

he wished that his life could just be done
so he closed his eyes, and dreamed himself home

• • •

now here they lie, with love at last
their friends stand, reminiscing their past

he loved her and she loved him
but their families could never blend

so they vowed their love through eternity
with a love this special, how can it be

their families could never stand hand in hand
to erase the shame of what they had planned

with families so proud unable to change
they took their own lives and didn't complain

before this all happened, they co-wrote a note
"maybe this will help others, that's what we hope"

• • •

how many of us, have found ourselves there
and would be a number, without those who care
think of the sorrow and grief, we could erase
if we'd lend a hand, before it's too late!!!

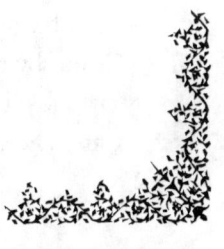

"Roll On Sweet River"

(for Tammy)

This next song I feel needs an explanation about
how I chose the name. Hopefully, this will suffice,
and serve as an introduction to "Roll On Sweet River."
These lyrics were transcribed from my tape recorder by a
gorgeous young lady from Ohio by the name of Tammy.
Tammy was very special to me, to say nothing of the fact
that my mother loved her very much and thought I should
marry her. Perhaps that would have worked for both of them,
however, I knew it would never work for me. But then,
we know everybody loves Tammy!!!

Tammy put this song on paper for me on our way to her home
in Akron Ohio. I wrote it for her on my way to her house
in Washington DC on August 12, 1965. It is now may the 11th
in the year of our Lord, 2015. Tammy left me with nothing
but beautiful memories, and by the way, she also had the most
beautiful handwriting I think I have ever seen. Perfect pen to
paper flow, with magnificent line structure and punctuation.
She was like an explosion of sensuality and sexiness, and that
included her handwriting. As I refer back to the dates on some
of my writings, that may just be the explanation for the many
breaks I took between some of my pieces. If it wasn't the reason,
perhaps it should have been. As I recall, Tammy always provided
all the best reasons for taking a break!!!

Tammy performed all of her duties to perfection. From her
job as a Sec. to a rather high ranking official in the C I A,
to fixing her hair, to the close she wore, to cooking, and last,
but by no means least, making me happy!!! It seems Tammy
was just born to please. She was very conscientious, enthusiastic
and cheerful, so soft and easy on your eyes. She was the perfect

[Roll on sweet River continued]

fit for a [moody] poet or songwriter lost in time, and always searching for a rhyme. I missed her then as I her now, I loved her then as I love her now. I describe her with two words in mind, though many others may apply.

Tammy, you were "So Fine"!!!

The riverboat was called the Dandy, it made evening dinner and party reservation cruises on the Potomac River. Providing a view of Washington DC and Fort Washington Maryland on one side, while the other side served you with Arlington, Alexandria, and Mount Vernon, Virginia. Tammy was really the only thing sweet about a Potomac River cruise, hence the title of the song.
"Roll On Sweet River"
roll on Sweet River, take me to my love
roll on Sweet River, she's all I'm dreaming of

roll on Sweet River, just like you have before
take me to my baby, and she'll be mine for evermore

well I've been searching far and wide
just to find a little girl to be my bride

now I finally found one, here's what she's worth
Sweet River take me, to my heaven on earth

there is an Angel here, you know what I mean
she came sailing in, on that old River Queen

when I get there--- I'm going to take off some time
you know I'm gonna--- make that sweet thing mine

[Roll on sweet River continued]

so roll on Sweet River---take me to my baby's arms
I'm gonna take her by the hand---and get lost in her charms

now there was a time---when I was happy by myself
but this old River---makes me want someone else

so roll on Sweet River---like you never rolled before take me to my
lady---and I won't bother you no more

just the slightest touch---from her hand
makes her every wish---my command

she says sweet nothings---and my heart skips
and you know she's got---the sweetest lips

so roll on Sweet River, oh here me when I say
take me to my Angel---and that is where I'll stay
Ro-l-l On-----Swe---et Ri---ver!!!

Tammy, I hope you are well, and life has been good
to you
I hope you enjoyed me, just half as much as I
enjoyed you
Your MKV Productions
master of ceremonies
love you baby
Keith

"Scrambled"

*but for the power to read one's mind
thoughts and wishes of all kind*

*a kind-a mixed up mass of jumbled dreams
of which the end or truth is far unseen*

*troubled minds, unscrambled thoughts
accompanied by half-pieced together dreams*

*appearing as though they are in tact
as a part of some un-thought of scheme*

*but yet 'tis I who thought of this
which must be my final feat*

*'tis for thee I live, and thee I die
if choice be my treat*

*choice, oh I speak of this, how could I dare
when naught is left of such*

*choice, I had this same, 'twas at a time
when life meant more than much*

*but hence the comforter hath come forth
to wrappeth tight my brain*

*has locked inside the scrambled memory's
as though to shelter from the rain*

*why shelters such a mangled mess
of mis-fit thoughts thou doth caress*

[Scrambledcontinued]

*why not permit they burst with glee
from truth that's buried deep in thee*

*once again I hear a different word
'tis one that not so many heard*

*truth, aw--truth is for the very few
that to themselves can say, I'm true*

*you, not you, you have no right to use this word
for as yet, truth from you has not been heard*

*facts are more than truth to you
yet most facts are far from being true*

*facts are proven and misconstrued
so truth be known by chosen few*

*the truth is very hard to find
buried deep inside the mind*

*oh to see and maybe tell
what's in the mind, we know so well!!!*

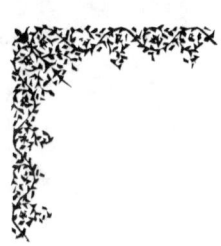

"70's Magic"

[sometime in the 70s]

have you not heard in years gone by
and present day as well

people singing songs of joy
and of love stories tell

oh how nice this is to hear
so cheerfully give praise

through winter, summer, spring and fall
'tis as though we're in a daze

we should all be thankful
for this land in which we live

be thankful for our natural freedom
of which others fought to give

for all of nature's beauty
many thanks we should afford

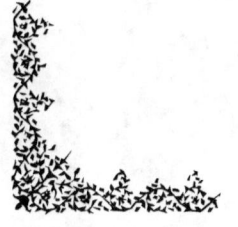

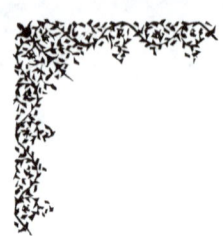

[70's magic continued]

for the luxury of dreaming
when we are tired and bored

just to lie out in the pasture field
and gaze upon a star

where horses roam and cattle graze
with no worries of where you are

we have an endless list of thankfulness
for friends, and work, or play

I am extremely thankful, these thoughts
took place in Great Falls, V a

"God", I love Virginia
she has always been my girl

there is no place I'd rather live
in this entire world

though I am not with her now
she guides my dreams at night

my thanks will still be to her
as I take my final flight!!!

"Shaking The Dust Off My Feet"

[song]

I'm shaking the dust off my feet, and I'll be leaving
I'm pulling out now honey, and I am not grieving

yeah, you're way behind me now
but I'll make out somehow

I'm not a worried man
I don't even have a plan

so I'll shake the dust off my feet
and my heart won't skip a beat

I'll be walking through that door
and you'll never see me no more
cause I'm shakin' that "ole" dust off my feet

there's no grass growing under my shoes
I got no time for----singing the blues

I got a lot of living to do before I die
so I'm shaken dust, and telling you goodbye

yes I'm shakin' the dust off my feet
I forgot about you when I hit the Street

you kept me hanging on too long
now you can call me gone

cause I'm shakin' that "ole" dust off my feet!!!

"She's A Real Good Friend Of Mine"

[song]

she can make me feel-- like million dollars
and takes me places-- that will make me holler
she's a party girl, with an afterglow
and she wears it well--every place she goes
oh no, she's not my woman, but she sure is fi-ne
and she-- is a friend of mine

well she calls me up, and says it's party time
and when she ar-rives, lawd she's looking fine
she has what it takes, to stand out in a crowd
and when she comes to m-e-e, she's walkin' proud
now she's not my woman, but she sure is fi-ne
and she--- is a friend of mine

she's right there with me, for the good and the bad
unlike some others, we all have had
there just ain't no way, to put a price on her
the only woman I knew, to always call me sir
now she's not my woman, aw but lawd knows she's fine
and she-e-e is a real good friend of mine!!!

"She's Special"

(for 2-27-45)

you're gone, you're gone, like Summers rose
should you return, in sweet repose

o call upon the one who knows
one whose loveless life doth show

all memory's mired with afterglow
to have possessed and then let go

you're gone, you're gone, yet you remain
with each breath I take and step I gain

for good or bad it's all the same
should my response be with refrain

you loved me much without complaint
but then, my true love I would taint

oh hold me near and ease my pain
prove times we shared were not in vain!!!

"Silhouette Sex"

(for my Lady D)

What an unselfish lover
to share her pleasures with others

if it only be through silhouette
it could enhance their enjoyment

with shades pulled and lighted room
the figures show, excitement blooms

news spreads through the neighborhood
late evening walks are always good

the only one to dare display this scene
makes me proud she is my Queen

You see happiness and faces glowing
it enriches you just for the knowing

how proud she was to project
our perfect love in silhouette!!!

"Stop Your Rambling And Runnin' Around"

[song]

you gotta stop your rambling, and stop your running around
you gotta stop your rambling, and stop your running around
if you don't stop rambling and a running, you're going to end up 6 feet down
you better stop being so crazy, and start trying to behave
you better cut out the crazies, and start trying to behave
if you don't stop the things you're doing, you'll end up in an early grave – – hey--now

come to your senses, quit jumpin' fences, and try to settle down
stop picking the peaches from other peoples tree, just because they're not around
lawd, if you don't stop rambling and a runnin', your gonna end up 6 feet down--- a-yodel-lay-hey-he-he-he!!!

"Taking My Heart Home To Die"

[song]

today I'm hanging up your picture
to take its place among my memories
I will love you forever, that is true
but I must live my life for things that used to be

I cry until my tears are dry
when I think about the night we said goodbye
I know you don't love me, but I don't know why
so I'm taking my poor heart home to die

I am leaving this place as soon as I can
I'll go back home where I belong
for the loss of you was trouble, it gave me
unhappy memory's to take home
yes I'm letting you go
but I want you to know
before I say goodbye
I was much too blind to see
that losing you was killing me
so I'm taking my heart home to die!!!
(Feel sorry for me dammit)

"Teenage Fever"

[song]

well it's the teenage fever, turnin' loose of the past
yeah it's the teenage fever, man it's spreadin' fast

well they love to dance, and they love to shake
but eu--ee baby, when they quiver and quake
they got the teenage fever, from head to toe
and they want to give the fever, to everyone
they know

they've got hot rod cars, and act real cool
and they all drive just like a fool
cause they got the fever
yeah the teenage fever, always on the run
with the teenage fever, havin' nothing but fun

well I got a gal, she is a real deal
when she gets the fever, she gives my heart a thrill
it's the teenage fever
yeah the teenage fever

now there's a boy in town – he's a real gone--cat
he wears a black leather jacket and a motorcycle cap
he's got the teenage fever
yeah the teenage fever

everything they wear, has just got to match
because their itchin', where they can't scratch
they got the fever, gotta lose their past
yeah it's the teenage fever, man it's spreadin' fast!!!

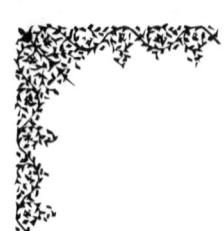

"To Gail"

oh Gail, such a lovely child
24 chasing 16 with a smile

I often wondered why life was so unfair
to birth a body and fill the mind with air

oh, and that body, what a body
it has become my favorite nightly toddy

it makes the conversation very clear
and tells me just why I'm here

letting me know you're only mine
throughout the night your love does shine

you're always on, and all aglow
born for the part, you really know

the mornings leave me in suspense
no sleep, no rest, no common sense!!!

"That Empty Feeling"

[song]
{for my wife}
now it's a mighty empty feeling
when you find your world reeling
and you know there's not a damn thing
you can do
hen your baby leaves you stranded
and you're feeling kind-a-branded
from a love that you thought always
would be true
yes there's something I've been missing
and I really need your kissing
I know that I have never been this blue
oh there's no need now for crying
for I feel just like I'm dying
I'm lost in memory's of your sweet
loving too
if you should ever change your mind
you know I won't be hard to find
I'll be living in the lobby of your heart
there's a phone right on the wall
if you feel like you should call
and tell me we can make another start
I keep trying to remember
what I did to make you ever
want to leave the love that we had
living here
was it something that I didn't do
that left an emptiness in you
if I knew, I would erase it--dear
cause it's a mighty empty feeling
when you find your world reeling
and you know there's not a damn—thing---you—can---do!!!

"The Awesome Oak"

this mighty Oak was my favorite tree
through many hot days it shaded me

when I was told that it must fall
'twas a very sad day as I recall

I conquered my feelings, cut it and cried
left feeling abandoned, and empty inside

what a "Great Tree," it should have never died
perfect in stature, spread 54 inches side to side

the pain I felt, showed clearly in my eyes
that same graceless feeling, experienced by the sky

never shall another come with such visual embrace
more than 100 years it stood in this same place

a lost and lonely look, lingered long upon my face
in the background I see, the sky has fell from grace!!!
"what-a-tree"

"The Big-B-Blues"

well the big B's got me "mama", worse than
anything I ever saw
yeah the big B's got me baby, beats
anything I ever saw
I gotta get me a beer, baby, would you get me a
beer, I'm gonna take a pause for the cause
hey--hey mama, listen to me honey, alright now,
you need to hear what your daddy say
I want to come home to you baby, but you got
to understand my ways

{A – yodel – lay – hey – he – he – he}
way down in Carolina baby, I'm just bummin' round
on the beach
yeah--down in Carolina honey, bummin' round
baby – just hangin' out on the beach
trying to heal my body baby
keepin' that "ole" beer bottle out of reach
{Ba – Baum – Ba – Baum – Baum – Baum – pretty baby}
hey now
{A – yodel – lay – hey – he – he – he}
yeah the big B's got me baby, it's gonna take
your daddy home
that "ole" big B's got your honey, it's gonna
bring your daddy home
now if you want me pretty mama, understand
where I'm coming from y—e—a—h
just fill your refrigerator baby, with Michelob
light
I may die from consumption, but I'll keep you happy all night
hey now – yes I will – you – know I will

[The big B blues continued]

yeah that big B's got your daddy, it's got me
worse than anything I ever saw
yeah the big B's got me mama, but if you want me,
all you gotta do is call – yeah – yeah
oh I'm headed back to DC pretty mama, and try
to get my head on right
coming back to DC honey, and screw it down
nice and tight
hey hey, listen to me now, if I don't find you
there waitin'
you know that "ole" big B's gonna take me South
listen to me baby – aw – hear me now – hear my call
yeah I love you pretty mama, but I love that big B
most of all – hey – hey
just fill your refrigerator baby, with Michelob
light
I may die from consumption, but I'm gonna keep
you happy all night
yeah – yeah – yeah you know I will, there ain't
no one like me{baby}
just give me a case or two mama, and I can be
anything you want me to be
{A – yodel – lay – hey – he – he – he}

oh I'm a well-traveled "daddy", been all over town
yeah I'm a well-traveled "Poppa", known all over this
town
so if you get lost mama, just call me up and
I'll show you around
oh the big B's got me honey, got your daddy
where it hurts
hey – that "ole" big B's got me baby, got me
right where it hurts
but I got a be moving on pretty baby, gotta get out

[The big B blues continued]

from under your skirt –{up out-a the dirt} y—e—a—h

just fill your refrigerator baby, with Michelob
light
I may die from consumption but I'll keep you
happy all night
{oh yes I will – Ba – Baum – Ba – Baum – Baum—Ba}

now when I die honey, put a funnel in my grave
[that's right baby] put that "ole" funnel down in my grave
and I'll have a drink with you mama, any time you pass
my way, yes I will – all right – well, I've enjoyed it mama
all the time I spent with you
hey – hey, had a great time pretty baby
spendin' my time with you
I guess all I got to say is, I'm glad that Big B don't have
you too
aw – take it away now
[**lower tone – – – stretch out**]
take it away baby, take it away
as far as you can go, yeah, take it baby
take it as far as you can go
but no matter what you do honey, try to take it
nice and slow
think about me mama, think about me
now and then
cause someday pretty baby, you're gonna
appreciate all the places we have been
{yeah baby, every – one – of – them}
{A – yodel – lay – hey – he – he – he}
aw that big B's got me mama, there's nothing
I can do
I'd like to tell you honey, I'd spend all my time
with you – but it ain't true – no it ain't true

[The big B blues continued]

that "ole" big B's got me baby, turned me into
a slave
yeah the big B's got me mama, turned your daddy
into a slave
every time I pick up that bottle honey, I just get
closer to my gra---ve ye-ah ye-ah
{A – yodel – lay – hey – he – he – he}
oh the big B's got me baby, brought me down
to my knees
yeah the big B's got me mama, way down – low
on my knees
I'm caught between the bottles baby, in a
Alcohol--lic squeeze
so get ready honey, let's rack it up one more
time
yet cut it loose baby, let's tear it up one last
time
make us another memory pretty mama, before
I cross over that line
just fill your refrigerator baby, with Michelob
light
daddy's gonna make you happy honey, if it takes
me all night
hey the big B's got your daddy, yeah it's got
your daddy bad
that "ole" big B's got me mama, and "la--awd"
it hurts so bad
but we've got good memories baby, ain't no
reason – to be sad
so good night mama, lay your dad-dy down
yeah good night pretty baby, wont you just –
lay "ole" Poppa down
I'm gettin' real tired – Sweet Mama – and
I think I wanna go home now

[The big B blues continued]

{A – yodel – lay – hey – he – he – he}
I guess it's the only way to lo-se these
"B-I-G – – B – –B-L-U-E-S"
{A – yodel – lay – hey – he – he – he}
"see you later baby"!!!

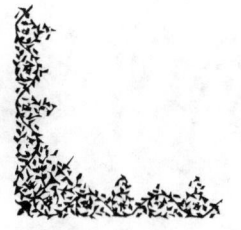

"The Loves Of Mr. V"

they began with my mother
and ended with you

to all of my loves
my heart has been true

I loved every one of them
but some I loved longer

my need for each would show when
I felt that I should become stronger

never, was one born to last
forever yearning to be free

brought latent pictures from my past
of what has become a memory

to see the rise of life's autumn sun
with empty arms, yet heart so full

cannot compare to cheers, well done
yet lays claim to their magnetic pull

to share the world from whence they rule
yes, I loved them all, when love was full!!!

"The Un-Gambler"

[recital/song]

This piece was written while making deliveries from Damascus Maryland, in route to Snow Hill Maryland. Just another hard-luck, fact of life!

[Chorus]
well gambling's just not my sport
when I play the horses they always run short
I play the numbers 15 at a time
but the one that comes out, comes in between mine
no, gambling's just not my game
that "ole" deck of cards, lawd's like an old flame
they haunt me and taunt me, time and again
seems like when I'm dreaming
is the only time I can win

now I bet on a cock fight, it seemed like a sure thing
an old friend of mines bird, had never been winged
he was a good-looking bird, so I put money on his side
and that damned "ole" cock, had a heart attack an died

well I was in my hometown for its 100th birthday
just boozin' with some old friends, when I heard someone say
there's a frog jumping contest this evening at five
I could feel my blood boiling, my heart came alive
I bet on this one frog, a fine--strong young bull
but when the gun went off, he looked like a damn fool
he stood straight-up and croaked, and then jumped with 2 feet
just a frog-hair behind, the front runnin' female
that just came in heat

[The un-gambler continued]

[chorus]
well gambling's just not my sport
when I play the horses they always run short
I play the numbers 15 at a time
but the one that comes out, comes in between mine
no, gambling's just not my game
that "ole" deck of cards, lawd's like an old flame
they haunt me and taunt me, time and again
it seems like when I'm dreaming is the only time I can win

now I figured just once before my life was through
my luck would have to change, and my Gamblin' too
they say unlucky at cards, and lucky at love
I figured with my luck, I'd need someone from above
so I'd been searching all day for this heavenly body
I had grown kind-a-tired, so I stopped for a toddy
then what to my tired weary eyes did appear
but the girl of my dreams, sitting sippin' a beer
well I choked on my toddy, to speak was a task
and I drank some more courage, then I walked up
and asked
oh lady, my lady, my lovely young lass
would you permit me the pleasure to kiss your
sweet—ask--
me no questions, and I'll tell you no lies
if you ever get hit with a bucket of sshh--bleep
be sure to close your eyes

[The un-gambler continued]

I don't know what happened, or what went wrong
but I had to resort to the only language I had known
so I said, "I'll put a C- note
on your petticoat
a-half-a-G-under your Pearl
lawd I'll lay a grand
in the palm of your hand
if—n' you'll be my girl
I'll hang at check
around your pretty neck
give your Boo-ga-loo
an I. O.U.
lawd I'll make you a mill
if I can drink my fill
from your fountain of youth
ba-doo-de-doo-doo"
and she said, "well, my name is Madge
and here's my badge
I've been waiting here for men like you
you got a way with words
like I have never heard
and I'd like to see what you could do
I sure liked it fine when you laid down your line
in fact I think it's swell, aw, but like it or not
you have just been caught
you've got to spend a little time in jail."
well it finally happened, I bet on a female
and if my luck stays true, it's easy to tell
if I bet on heaven, I'd wind up in hell

[The un-gambler continued]

[chorus]
no gambling's just not my sport
when I play the horses they always run short
I play the numbers 15 at a time
and the one that comes out, comes in between mine
oh gambling's just not my game
that "ole" deck of cards, lawd's like an old flame
they haunt me and taunt me, time and again
seems like when I'm dreaming
is the only time I can win!!!

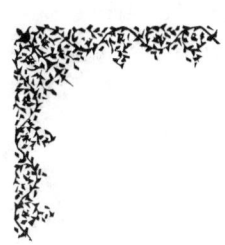

"Thee I Love"

(For my wife, Kathy)

aw 'tis true, it is thee I love
known to you for years

but uncovered by my senses
only now, in these days of wear

to be alone without your love
now in my mind, spreads a fear

to have thee not in times of need
gives my eyes cause to tear

could I have missed love's meaning
because you were always near

was I blinded by ambition
and not thinking very clear

now tomorrow yearns, for your gifted ear
life's winter, will be (oh) so cold, without you dear!!!

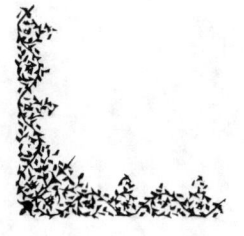

"They Need Me"

your memories have stopped haunting me
they only show up here for my company

so I don't feel alone, when I'm by myself
it's hard to be lonely, if there is someone else

I have loved you so much for so many years
your memory's need me to provide them cheer

your memory don't care, who holds you tight
they only know I held you, when things were right

they drop by every night and knock on my door
just because they miss what they had before

sometimes I'm having coffee or watching TV
in walks your memory cause it needs company

I don't mind at all, for it feels more like home
we have a glass of champagne so I don't drink alone

sometimes your memory drinks a little too much
and leans on my shoulder just looking for touch

every now and then, because of "ole" Dom
they climb in my bed, when the champagne is gone

their lonesome for love with the mood of the night
and searching for a time when everything was right

I can't blame them at all, I know how they feel
together we reminisce, about a love that was real

[They need me continued]

I don't go anywhere and I'll never leave town
they need my attention when they come around

and that's quite all right, I don't want to be free
I love all your memory's, and I know they need me!!!

"This Land Of "God's", And Ours"

I have no doubt that "God" shall tell
his purpose for this land so well

the mark of a prosperous nation we hold
with its liberty and freedom far untold

United together as one great state
50 of the same will lock its gate

throughout the country its people are blessed
truly from the hand of "God", and nothing less

a nation such as this shall never know defeat
for the touch of "God's" hand is impossible to beat

"God" made us as we are, and this way shall we be
our need is not for weapons of war to kill the enemy

the love of "God" is a greater gift, than a victory brought home
for the Bible tells us "God", will take care of his own!!!
(HE LIVES)

"Tired Of Being So Accused"

[song]

I'm tired of being so accused
I give you good love, you give me abuse
the way you treat me is a shame
yet somehow I get the blame

and I'm tired of being so accused

you al—ways think that I am untrue
but you--don't know—how I love you
your lack of faith in me is wrong
still my love for you is strong

and I'm tired of being so accused

if I did all the things you think I do
I'd be-e-e the busiest man in town
but I don't, and darling that's the truth
you're the only one I want to be around

but I'm tired of being so accused

honey i--f you don't believe, the things I say
I wonder how we'll ever make our way
you think – I'm just like all the rest
but the rest – don't have – the best

[I'm tired of being so accused continued]

I know exac--tly what I have in you
that's why I don't do – the things you think I do
I could ne-ver betray your trust that way
no mat--ter what your friends might say

I'm tired of being so accused

ev-erybo--dy says you are a fool
and they--know I will be untrue
what will-it take-to make you see
you are what makes my-life complete

but I'm tired of being so accused

what makes--you think that I would lie
to chance lo-s-ing you I'd rather die
how much more---must you put me through
before you see--my love for you is true

oh, I'm tired of being so accused

you know---I want a life for us
for that to happen we---must have trust
I pray someday--you'll know my love is true
then I can just---get down to loving you

for darling that--is all I want to do
but I'm so tired
yes, I'm tired of being so accused!!!

"Think Of The Memory's"

[song]

think of---the memory's that you'd have with me
but don't try---to hold me cause I want to be free

oh it's nothing you've done, it's what matters you see
but think of---the memory's, you could have with me

yeah think of---the memory's we could make together
ten years---down the road--with no stormy weather

but don't cou-nt on staying, that cou-ld never be
just think of---the memory's you'd have with me

I know---you love me, and I can feel that you care
honey I fe-el your heartbreak, when I hold you near

knowing you can't change, my desir--e to be free
but darling think of---the memory's you'd have with me
[end with chorus]
aw baby, think of -- the memory's we could make together
honey ten years---down the road, and no stormy weather
oh but don't try--to tie me, for I'll always be free
but just think of---the memory's you could have with me
("think about it baby")!!!

"This "Ole" Show"

[song]

this "ole" show has been a long time coming
it got started sixty years ago
I got side tracked about 100 times
made a lot of wrong turns, going to and fro

yeah this "ole" show has been a long time coming
but it'll be around for a day or so
I had to live it, before I played it
it was so much fun, I couldn't let it go
*** So if you like it***
You got-a let us know

"Three Chords A Teardrop And A Bottle Of Beer"

[song]
the song was written for my uncle Ray Stoneking.
In the mid-60s, His home was where me and his son Jimmy, and several
other musicians, would regularly hold jam sessions. Three chords
was all uncle Ray knew. But after a case of beer and a bottle
of Jack Daniels or Jim Beam, he didn't need to know anymore.
He could put those three chords together just like Chet Adkins or
Roy Clark and we made some pretty good sounds. People would
come by to join in until the wee hours in the morning from
all around, hence the title of the song.

Well it's three chords, a teardrop, and a bottle of
beer
my life is so empty, it seems like the end is
near
I fell off all my bridges, and it's bottoms-up from
here
give me three chords, a teardrop, and a bottle of
beer

three chords, a teardrop, and a bottle of beer
I was looking for fame and fortune, they said
I could find it here
but I must've zigged when I should have zagged
cause it is very clear
there's no fame and fortune, only three chords,
a teardrop, and a no good bottle of beer

[Three chords a teardrop and a bottle of beer continued]

you must understand the mindset, you get from
living here
temptations always present, when there's nothing
left to fear
it's just three chords, a teardrop and a bottle of
beer
yeah, three chords, a teardrop, and a no good bottle
of beer
when you put them all together, you can get lost
for years
with a cheatin' wife and a wasted life, there's very
little cheer
with three chords, a teardrop, and a damned "ole"
bottle of beer
[chorus]
now it's three chords, a teardrop, and a bottle of
beer
I fell off all my bridges, and it's bottoms-up from
here
no time to waste, I need a taste, to help me find
a tear
then I'll have three chords, a teardrop
and a damned "ole" bottle-a-beer!!!

"Tryin' To Fall"

some people say I'm lucky
but I don't understand that at all

I been sitting here waiting for my baby
and she don't even call

my car broke down this morning
and I'll be bankrupt by fall

but they still say I'm lucky
yeah, the luckiest man they ever saw

I guess they don't get around much
I think they're completely out-a-touch

I just feel like I ought to get drunk
sit down and write a country song

maybe I can write one about bad luck
or about some woman doin' me wrong

I guess no one wants to bother
with the star that's tryin' to fall

or maybe they think I'm so lucky
I just don't need any help at all

I don't know where they get that idea
unless they're deaf, dumb, and blind

the way my luck is, if I raced a turtle
it would probably leave me behind

[Tryin' to fall continued]

sometimes I wonder just what they had to smoke
I wouldn't feel so bad if someone else was broke

I've been playing that damned "ole" lotto
for so long I can't remember when

and the way those numbers keep fallin'
it looks like it'll be that long again

sometimes I start feeling lucky
and I think I'm about to win

then fate punches a hole in my bubble
as the numbers start rolling in

I got caught speeding through radar
and wound up on the bad side of the law

the IRS is looking for me
I've got no place left to crawl

but they still say I'm lucky, just to be alive
so I guess I should be happy, as long as I survive!!!

"Unhappy Day"

this must be an unhappy day
there is nothing going my way

the older I get, the more foggy my mind
I think of the past, and memories are blind

yes, this must be, an unhappy day
I guess for my birth, today I must pay

it seems somewhere I lost my way
and I am left with very little to say

I am forced to acknowledge this day of the year
but each year it comes accompanied by fear

fear of time and the timeline of life
the nearing of death cuts like a knife

I have enjoyed all my days on this earth
still, an unhappy day, is the day of my birth!!!

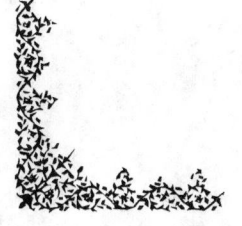

"Unnamed"

there was only one man of sonnets
but many men of grief

waiting for a heart to break
so they could write relief

the more heartaches, the better
the lines portrayed the thief

with structure to the poems
that restricted one's belief

yet as a sonnet blossoms
intrigue and interest grow

inviting the story's ending
to what we think we know

leaning hard towards unreal
the end shares collective zeal!!!

"Wars! Wars!"

(Why must they be)

from the far shores of the ocean
to the highest mountaintop

we hear the cries of agony
"why can't these wars be stopped"

one half the world is fighting for freedom
while the other half fights to gain control

when in the end man cannot win
lest he lose his immortal soul

Wars! Wars! – Why must they be?
these words leaves one haunted

still some fight for freedom rights
while others remain undaunted

is it not an endless venture
this quest for world peace

wars have been, and wars still are
and wars, shall never cease

isn't it enough to have
our own lives to live

why must we strive to conquer
instead, why can't we give

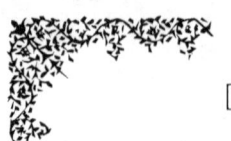

[Wars wars why must they be--- continued]

"Wars! Wars! – Why must they be?"
as through the bloody battlefields we trod

is it so now, that we have not
either love, nor fear of "God"

have we lost our very teachings
as we fight with all our will

His commandments tell us
it is not right to kill

yet still the march goes on
for this hopeless victory

a guarantee of the life we live
shall be of endless misery

oh, Wars!! Wars!! – Why must they be?
The answer remains unknown

the dead and wounded numbers mount
and we are mindless, to what we have been shown!!!

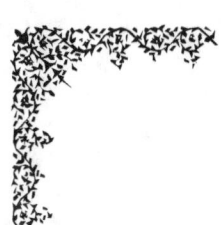

"We Need A Home"

yes my love we need a home
a simple place to call our own
it doesn't have to be a Castle
just someplace free of hassle

oh there are things we must discuss
I hope that won't be a problem for us
don't let memory's stand in your way
and then perhaps we both can stay

if it gets rough I'll pack my gear
perhaps I shall not shed a tear
yes my love – we need a home
to give us both a comfort zone

a place apart from all distraction
where we can bathe in satisfaction!!!

"Weeping"

weeping is a feeling from the heart and of the mind
compassion for someone or something we find
could be caused by pain, happiness, or even glory
maybe someone or something from yesterday's story
crying comes from pain or abuse one receives
either to their person or to one of their properties
an emotion from the mind not really of the heart
physical, mental, monetary loss, will play a part
sometimes we cry from emptiness, if time is cheap
almost everybody cries, but few people weep!!!

"What Am I Going To Do"

I remember the times when I was happy
not a teardrop or heartache could be found

now things have changed the tears fall free
and there's heartache all around

I know I've done so many things
that a true love should never do

so late it be, I understand
the things I put you through

left with lonely lines and shadows
that crawl my walls each night

breaching sun begins with thoughts of you
and questions, can I ever make it right

how could I have forsaken your love so true
oh, tell me darling, what am I going to do???

"Willow Winds"

the wind that blows the Willow
is gentle as it flows

and the waves of the Willow
swing softly to and fro

the Willow waiting for the wind
its branches waving without end

and when it leaves, its only yearn
is for the wind, but to return

the Willow tree must love the wind
they are truly two of nature's friends

while being dauntless to its force
the Willow lets the wind take course

and away the wind blows from above
Willow waves goodbye to its natural love!!!

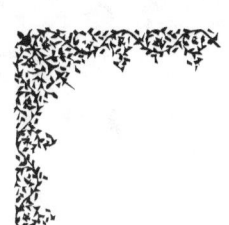

"Your Wedding Day"

I could not attend your wedding
though I watched it from afar

with every dance and kiss I saw
put a hole right through my heart

I don't know why you invited me
when you own my heart and soul

was it a message that you sent
to make me lose control

or was it just your way of saying
that you don't love me anymore

with no concern of feelings on my part
no goodbyes, just a dagger to the core

I know my love will linger, and endure the pain
though it would be much easier, just to go insane!!!

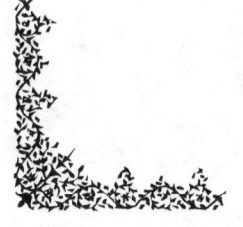

www.ingramcontent.com/pod-product-compliance
Lightning Source LLC
Chambersburg PA
CBHW052055070526
44584CB00017B/2186